Original title:
Frosted Trails and Snowy Paths

Copyright © 2024 Creative Arts Management OÜ
All rights reserved.

Author: Henry Beaumont
ISBN HARDBACK: 978-9916-94-556-8
ISBN PAPERBACK: 978-9916-94-557-5

Paths Entwined with Silver Lace

Little feet slip and slide,
Watch the tumble, what a ride!
Snowmen wobble, hats askew,
Even penguins laugh—who knew?

Sleds flip over, laughter spills,
Hot cocoa waits, the warmth fulfills.
Snowballs flying—dodge and weave,
Best to plan a quick reprieve!

The Quiet Dance of Falling Snow

Snowflakes twirl like ballerinas,
Landing softly on our witnesses.
Chasing cats in cozy mitts,
As they sneak up—oh, the hits!

Puppies leap with sheer delight,
Chasing shadows in the night.
We slip and slide, oh what a jam,
I swear I'll never live this down, ma'am!

Uncharted Routes in Frost's Embrace

Maps made of ice look so classy,
Take a turn and hope you're not trashy.
Lost and found in white confusion,
The path's a laugh, just an illusion!

Parks are filled with snowball fights,
Giggles echo in the chilly nights.
Finding warmth in each snowdrift,
Perhaps a hot tub would be a gift?

A Tapestry of Ice and Solitude

Winter evenings, hot tea brewing,
But outside? A blizzard—who's pursuing?
Neighbors shout with icy cheer,
As snowflakes welcome us with beer!

Lonely squirrel in a hat so grand,
Giving side-eye to the frosty land.
Down the street, a snowman smiles,
With carrots for noses and plaid styles!

Wings of Snowflakes in Twilight Air

Snowflakes dance like tiny sprites,
They twirl and swirl, free of all fights.
One lands on my nose, a chilly surprise,
Like a little snowball, a prank in disguise.

I catch one in my mittened hand,
A slippery trick, just like planned.
It melts away, a giggle in air,
As I ponder life in this frosty affair.

Signs of Life Beneath the Frost

Under the ice, the squirrels just dream,
Of summer's nuts, their favorite theme.
They poke their heads, with snowflakes aglow,
Looking quite shocked at the winter show.

A rabbit hops by, wearing a scarf,
He stops for a moment, gives a good laugh.
"Why so serious?" he winks with a flick,
"Enjoy this chill, make it your trick!"

A Footstep's Path Through Winter's Heart

Every footstep crunches with mirth,
Sound of giggles echoes the earth.
I slipped on a patch, oh what a sight,
I waved like a penguin, quite full of fright.

A snowman watches, with a carrot nose,
But so very still, he forgot how to pose.
A hat ill-fitted, his buttons amiss,
Between joy and chaos, he finds his bliss.

Dappled Sunlight on a Frozen Road

Sunshine peeks through a curtain of white,
It makes the cold morning feel just right.
A dog skids past, on a wild snow chase,
With a bark of surprise, and boundless grace.

A child swings snowballs, aiming so bold,
Missed the mother, but hit the old mold.
Laughter erupts as the moments unfold,
In this winter wonder, humor's pure gold!

Beneath the Icicle-Dripped Canopy

Icicles hang like chandeliers,
A frozen feast for snowy deers.
I slipped on ice, oh what a sight,
Like Bambi tripped in broad daylight!

My mittens lost in white delight,
Snowballs fly, we shout and fight.
The sun peeks out, the snow looks sly,
It winks at us, oh why oh why!

A Portrait of Peace in White

A snowman stands with a crooked grin,
He looks like me after too much gin!
His carrot nose is slightly bent,
Just like my plans, ill-spent and spent!

With playful grins, we roll the flakes,
Laughter echoes, as balance breaks.
In this wintry world, we dance and prance,
Our clumsy steps, a snowy romance.

Echoes of Laughter in the Snow

Whispers of snow, oh what a sound,
As we tumble and roll, all over the ground.
A snowball fight, oh what fun,
Face full of snow, I can't even run!

Hot cocoa spills, marshmallow globs,
We drink and laugh, like silly mobs.
The world is white, a fluffy kite,
In this winter wonder, everything feels right.

Winter's Palette of Stillness

The trees wear coats of frosty white,
Like fashion models, posing right.
But then a branch drops, oh dear me,
Now I'm stacked like a domino tree!

Footprints dance in a snow-white trance,
Each step a silly, frosty prance.
The world feels calm, yet filled with cheer,
In this blanketed joy, we have no fear.

Threads of Silence on a Winter's Walk

Crunch and crack with every step,
Silent snowflakes jest and prep.
My boots are big, my heart's a kite,
Wobbling around like a solo fright.

Dancing squirrels give me a stare,
Do they think I'm a snowman rare?
I trip on ice, a slippery sight,
Laughing echoes through the chilly night.

Secret Paths in a Hidden Glade

Where are we off, my little feet?
Following rabbits on a frosty cheat.
They hop and giggle, what a game!
While I tumble and roll, oh such shame!

The trees are whispering, 'Take it slow!'
But laughter falls like soft-driven snow.
A fox takes a peek, with a sly little grin,
As I wrestle with boots 'neath the winter's skin.

The Last Whisper of Autumn's Breath

Leaves turned to snow, what a cruel joke!
A chilly wind gives an icy poke.
I chase a leaf that's dressed so fine,
But it slides away like it's on divine line.

A last hurrah before the freeze,
I jog with style, but where's the ease?
With each mishap, my laughter's shared,
As branches shake and woodland's bared.

Radiant Silence of the Winter Night

Stars blink down like giggling sprites,
Wrapped in this blanket of snowy whites.
I build a fort that looks like a blob,
And wonder if a snowball can lob!

Penguin waddle across the yard,
Neighbors peek out, it feels quite charred.
Will snowmen rise and take their throne?
Or will they melt and leave me alone?

Snow-laden Boughs and Creaking Branches

Boughs weighed down with icy fluff,
Squirrels in boots, oh that's enough!
Laughter crackles in the frosty air,
As penguins slide without a care.

Creaking branches tell their tales,
Of snowmen stuck in silly trails.
With carrot noses, oh so grand,
They plan a dance, hand in hand!

The Crystal Path to Dreams Unseen

A path of crystals, shiny and bright,
Where children stumble, what a sight!
They twirl and whirl, slip and fall,
Chasing snowflakes, a free-for-all.

Snowballs fly, oh what a mess,
A battle rages, can you guess?
Face full of snow, laughter's embrace,
Who knew winter had such a face!

Tales Told by Moonlight on a Snowy Lane

Under the moon, tales take flight,
Of snowmen plotting in the night.
A rabbit hops in a stylish hat,
While a wise old owl just laughs at that.

They gather round for a snowy feast,
With marshmallow treats, oh what a beast!
The frost brings giggles, fun, and cheer,
As dreams of hot cocoa draw near.

Murmurs Beneath the White Blanket

Beneath the blanket, whispers thrive,
Squirrels discuss how to survive.
Wanderers trip, oops! What a slip,
Even the snowman lets out a quip.

Laughter bubbles from the trees,
As winter throws its wildest tease.
With every gust, a joke takes flight,
In this chilly, merry delight!

Threads of Warmth in a Chilling Realm

In coats so thick, we waddle about,
Like penguins lost, with nary a shout.
Our hats sit low, covering our eyes,
While snowflakes plop like playful spies.

We trip on mounds, and giggles abound,
The chill in the air has laughter unbound.
With cheeks so red, we dash and dive,
Each slip a reminder we're still alive!

A Journey Beyond the Flurry

We set out on foot, with no aim in sight,
Chasing fluffy clouds that dance in delight.
Snowballs take flight, a soft, icy rage,
Just your luck, you're now on the stage!

With every step, the crunch is like music,
Our laughter erupts, it's all rather comic.
We build a snowman with a crooked grin,
As frosty gusts stir up giggles within.

The Frozen Symphony of Calm

The world's a canvas, in white and blue,
Where every flake seems to dance, so true.
We bring our spoons, for a scoop of delight,
Ice cream from clouds in this frosty bite.

A penguin parade wobbles on by,
Each time they slip, we let out a cry.
With cocoa in hand, we cheer and tease,
A chill in the air, but we've got the keys!

Nature's Quiet Embrace in the Cold

In the hush of the snow, the world feels small,
We tumble and fumble, with grace we stall.
A snowman resembles a marshmallow puff,
With buttons for eyes, it's never enough!

With gloves on our paws, we frolic with glee,
Penguin slides beckon, "Come play with me!"
The warmth of our laughter, a spark in the freeze,
In this whimsical land, we do as we please!

Where the Silver Foxes Roam in White

In the woods where the air is brisk,
Foxes dance, their tricks quite a whisk.
With coats so bright, they prance and slide,
Chasing their tails, oh what a ride!

Snowballs thrown by cheeky crows,
As frosty winds, a cold wind blows.
They poke their heads from under piles,
And flash silly grins, wearing snowflakes' wiles.

Squirrels chatter, debating their stash,
While slipping and sliding, oh what a crash!
The whole forest giggles, holding its breath,
As winter's whimsy plays with them, no less!

Through all the laughter, a rumble ensues,
As snowmen gather, with brightly dressed shoes.
They wobble and wobble, but never fall flat,
Except when a fox steals a carrot hat!

The Quiet Magic of a Winter Night

Under the stars in a blanket of white,
Snowflakes dance, what a whimsical sight!
A penguin waddles, a clumsy charmer,
He slips on ice, his balance a drama!

The owls hoot softly, as if in a jest,
While rabbits are hopping, they can't seem to rest.
Tails twitching wildly in playful delight,
They leave tiny pawprints, a puzzling sight.

Nearby a snowman, quite proud of his hat,
Sways to the rhythms of a breeze just like that.
His carrot nose twitches with tickling glee,
As children dash by with snowballs in spree!

The moon winks cheekily from high above,
Spreading joy silently, like a warm hug.
So let's raise a toast to the wintery cheer,
Where laughter and snowflakes bring fun all year!

Journeying into the Land of Ice

In winter's grip, we slip and slide,
With snowflakes dancing, we laugh with pride.
A snowman winks with a carrot nose,
As we tumble down and our laughter grows.

The penguins tease, they waddle with glee,
While we try to ski—oh, look at me!
A face plant awaits, as I flail around,
Covered in snow, I'm the talk of the town.

Where Dreamers Tread in Crystal Dust

The snowflakes twirl like a dizzying dance,
With each fluffy step, we take a chance.
Hot cocoa in hand, my mittens get stuck,
I'm part snowman now, oh what bad luck!

A squirrel dashes by, with a nut in its grasp,
While I drop my drink, loud gleeful gasp.
But laughter is wrapped in the chilly embrace,
Friends in the snow, it's a stunning space.

Below the Silent Canopy of Snow

The trees are all dressed in white winter wear,
But watch out, my friend, for low-hanging hair!
A branch gives a smack, as I curl and I yawn,
I feel like a marshmallow, just floating along.

With snowball fights melting into pure fun,
A dodgy escape—nowhere left to run!
I slip on the ice, it's a theatrical dive,
They cheer that I'm here, they say I'm alive!

A Pathway to Frosted Fantasies

With frosty breath, we dash out the door,
Chasing each other, we're slipping—oh no more!
A snowdrift awaits like a soft pillow fight,
As we tumble and roll, what a silly sight!

Now snowmen are built with fantastic flair,
One looks quite grumpy, is he giving a stare?
But laughter erupts as we shove in a hat,
He finally smiles, imagine that!

Whispers of Winter's Veil

Snowflakes tango from the sky,
Sipping cocoa, oh my, oh my!
Slippery socks, a daring feat,
Twirl and slip, take a seat!

Winter's breath, a frosty tease,
Sneaky winds, they love to sneeze.
Snowman hats, all askew,
He's winking at me, how rude!

Silent Steps on a Winter Canvas

Puffy jackets, buttons pop,
Waddling like a little bop.
Snowballs fly, a cheeky fling,
Laughter echoes, it's a swing!

I built a fort, or so I thought,
But it's just a pile, I'm distraught.
My neighbor's ace, that snowball snare,
Oh no! That's ice cream, I swear!

Glimmering Footprints in the Moonlight

Moonbeams dance on frosty ground,
With each step, the crunching sound.
Tiny paws chase after me,
What's that? A snowman's cup of tea?

Lopsided hats on snowman pals,
It's as if they're having galas.
Giggling ghosts in snowy white,
Little hiccups in the night!

Chilling Echoes of a Frozen Dawn

Winter's laugh, a chilly blast,
A rogue mitt, lost in the past.
Frosty breath, I hop and skip,
A slippery dance—oh, what a trip!

Sneaky squirrels, plotting schemes,
A snowball fight? Oh, in my dreams!
Toboggans zoom, it's quite a show,
Whoops! There goes my hot cocoa!

The Elegance of a Whispering Breeze

A snowman winks with a carrot nose,
While snowflakes dance in wintry prose.
The old sled creaks with a joyful cheer,
As kids zoom past, their laughter near.

A penguin slips, does a funny dance,
Pops back up, gives ice skating a chance.
With frosty breath, the friends all shout,
Creating snow angels, giggling about.

Navigating Dreams in Winter's Grip

A cat in a scarf strolls around the block,
Catching a snowflake like it's a rock.
The dogs get tangled in their own leashes,
While snowballs fly, oh the happy breeches!

Hot cocoa spills as we dash for the door,
Slippers go flying, who can ignore?
The wind chimes jingle a frosty old tune,
As we dodge snowflakes that fall like a rune.

Shimmering Halls of Nature's Beauty

Icicles dangle from the old rooftop,
One leads to a drip with a comical plop.
Snow shovels battle, it's quite the scene,
As neighbors conspire for the best 'snow queen.'

But oh! The next step's a slippery fall,
A friendly reminder, winter's a brawl.
Yet through the laughter, we find our way,
Enjoying the frolics of a bright winter's day.

Shadows on the Ice-Covered Ground

A raccoon in boots checks his reflection,
Trying to skate with the utmost perfection.
He wobbles and twirls, oh what a sight,
Creating a show with his frosty delight.

While owls take bets on who'll fall first,
Snowmen all giggle; it's quite the burst.
But laughter erupts as they tumble en masse,
In this winter wonderland, fun's sure to amass.

Echoes of a Silent Snowfall

Snowflakes come down, a tickle, a tease,
They dance and they swirl in a cold winter breeze.
A face full of white, what a sight to behold,
As I slip on an icicle, feeling quite bold.

Sleds racing down, like a ride at the fair,
With snowballs a-flying, I'm locked in despair.
My hat's blown away, like it's taken a trip,
Just me and my laughter, and a possible slip.

The Frozen Embrace of Dawn

The sun peeks above, with a giggle and wink,
My coffee's all frozen, oh dear, what a drink!
I'm bundled in layers, a marshmallow puff,
But that penguin at play? He's showing me up.

I trudge through the sparkles, a march of pure glee,
But my boots are a riddle, all squishy and free.
In the snowI make angels, my wings look a mess,
Each flap sends a flurry—oh, winter's success!

Veils of Winter's Tender Touch

The world's wrapped in white, like a grand pastry treat,
But I'm slipping and sliding, just can't find my feet!
A snowman's my rival, with his buttons so bright,
I'm falling and laughing—oh, what a delight!

The trees wear their coats, all fluffy and nice,
But I lost my old scarf, now it's fashionable mice.
I trip on a twig, make a snow angel flop,
My friends laugh so loud, will this ever stop?

Shimmering Footprints in the Cold

A path of soft shimmer, my boots leave their mark,
I'm marching through snowflakes, a snow-covered park.
But who snuck a banana, right there on the way?
Now I'm doing a tango, in winter ballet!

The neighbors' cats giggle, they know all the tricks,
As I tumble and fumble amidst all the kicks.
With each crunchy step, my laughter unfolds,
In this land of the frosty, where joy never folds.

A Symphony of Frost and Shadows

In winter's grip, the snowmen dance,
Their carrot noses take a chance.
They wobble and sway with frosty cheer,
While snowballs fly from far and near.

Icicles hang like daggers sharp,
The squirrels play tunes on a frozen harp.
But watch your step on the icy lane,
Or you might just slip and sing in pain.

The snowflakes giggle, oh what a sight,
As they tickle noses, pure delight.
A snowman sneezes, causing a scene,
And laughter echoes, soft and keen.

Beneath the moon, shadows paint the ground,
While snow angels giggle without a sound.
With tangled scarves and mittens tight,
Winter becomes a comical plight.

Lanterns of Ice in the Dusk

Frozen lanterns hang from trees,
A nighttime party, if you please.
The ice glows bright with a chilly charm,
But don't get too close, it might cause harm.

Between the branches, shadows prance,
As frostbitten elves join in the dance.
They stumble and trip on their own two feet,
Creating a scene that's a frosty treat.

Snowflakes drift as if they tease,
Hitching a ride on the winter breeze.
A dog barks loudly, a ghostly howl,
And runs into snow, wearing a scowl.

Under the stars, the fun does grow,
With snowmen gossiping about the snow.
They laugh at penguins wearing a hat,
And share their gossip with a flurry and splat.

The Ghosts of Winter Wanderers

In the still of night, they roam the snow,
A jolly band of old friends, though.
With icy boots and whoopee cushions,
They glide along with comical wishes.

One trips on a branch, a comical flop,
While others chuckle, they just can't stop.
Snowflakes land on their chilled-up cheeks,
To tickle their noses, they laugh and squeak.

The moonlight casts a funny glow,
On their frosty antics, stealing the show.
They play hide and seek in piles so high,
With snowballs flying while giggles sigh.

So heed their laughter if you should pass,
For these winter ghosts are full of sass.
And if you trip in their gleeful fray,
Join in the fun, don't run away!

Departure Through a Sea of White

Packing up snacks under a snowy pine,
Laughter erupts like sparkling wine.
With mittens mismatched and boots untied,
Off on adventures, full of joy they glide.

A sled full of snacks, they trudge through white,
While a snowman watches with eyes so bright.
They race down slopes, oh what a ride,
With snow spray flying, all filled with pride.

Hot cocoa muffs in the frosty air,
Sip, slurp, and giggle without a care.
The path is absurd, but off they go,
In a world so silly, decorated in snow.

As they wave goodbye to their frosty friends,
With snowflakes dancing, the fun never ends.
In the laughter of winter, their hearts are light,
Through a blizzard of joy, they take flight.

The Calm After the Winter Storm

In boots too big, I waddle slow,
Snowflakes dance, oh look at them go!
My neighbor's cat slips, does a pirouette,
Tell him it's winter, not a ballet set!

The world is quiet, like a snoring bear,
Uncle Fred's stuck in a snowbank, oh dear!
Hot cocoa spills, my cup's on my knee,
I laugh so hard, the cat joins with me!

Sleds collide in a comical cheer,
Is it a snowy day or a sitcom premiere?
We're building a fort, but it looks like a blob,
Check out the mailman—he's part of the mob!

But once the sun glows, the fun fades away,
We munch on cookies, our hut's in disarray.
Snowmen salute us, slightly askew,
They might start a snowball war—who knew?

Celestial Footprints on a Starry Night

Stars above twinkle like holiday lights,
We stumble through snow, tripping on tights.
With every step, we leave prints of dough,
Did I just slip in a powdery show?

The moon's a big cookie, it makes me swoon,
In shadowy whispers, I hear a raccoon.
He's eyeing my snack with a mischievous grin,
Oh buddy, I'm sorry, it's too late for sin!

We walk hand in hand, with laughter and cheer,
Misguided by owls who hoot too near.
Slips and slides, what a chaotic ballet,
Next time I'll stick to indoor cupcake array!

But the snowy nights hold a magical charm,
Even if our faces are stuck in alarm.
A sprinkle of giggles and toppings of wit,
Dancing in moonlight, oh, we won't quit!

Ebon Pines Under a Silver Dome

Under the pines, I attempt a grand ski,
But I crash into bushes—oh, how could it be?
The trees say, "Ouch!" as I tumble in style,
Maybe they'll give me an award for a while?

The squirrels are chattering, plotting a heist,
While I build a snowman—not quite precise.
He's all lopsided, with a carrot that's bent,
Should I call him Mr. Wobbly or leave him unbent?

The night brings laughter, my friends join the spree,
One's stuck in a snowdrift, as happy as can be.
They'll have stories to tell, as they trudge back home,
With tales of the pines and our silly snow dome!

Under the silver dome, we frolic with glee,
Each flop and each fall is pure comedy.
The trees may chuckle, the stars may conspire,
Next winter's adventure, we might just retire!

The Winter's Tale of A Thousand Paths

In a world of white, where laughter erupts,
We trudge through snow, while the snowman disrupts.
He's lost his nose and a button or two,
All thanks to my dog, who just loves a chew!

Sliding on ice like I'm scaling a cliff,
My graceful moves would give anyone a myth.
Falling like a log, with an awkward spin,
I'll just tell folks that I danced on a whim!

The air is filled with giggles and sights,
Snowballs are flying in chaotic fights.
Friendship sealed tight with a thawing snow,
Who knew each snowflake could dance to our show?

The winter's tale whispers in all laughter,
With every adventure, there's always a chapter.
So gather your pals, let the tales unfold,
In a land of wonder, we'll be forever bold!

Reflections on a Paralyzed Landscape

A snowman wearing shades just stood,
He thought he'd take the winter good.
But when he tried to wave hello,
His arms fell off, much to his woe.

The trees wore coats, all snug and tight,
They whispered jokes in the pale moonlight.
A squirrel skated, slipped, and spun,
And landed face-first, we had good fun.

Every car turned into a sled,
With sleepy drivers, none got fed.
They all just laughed, 'round tables piled,
With cocoa mugs, we felt like children wild.

So here we sit, in winter's hold,
With tales of ice, both bright and bold.
As laughter echoes through the freeze,
We find our joy in snowball tease.

The Dance of Snowflakes in Twilight

A flake does twirl, then goes awry,
It lands right on a cat's poor eye.
The feline blinks, then jumps and runs,
While flakes laugh hard, oh winter funs!

Skiers crash in a puffy heap,
While snowmen giggle and then leap.
A penguin slides, "Not my best day!"
As he zips past in a snowy fray.

The streetlights blink, 'Is this a joke?'
While kids throw snowballs, purest smoke.
A snowball fight breaks out anew,
Faces all covered in white and blue.

So dance, dear flakes, 'neath dying light,
Let's make the best of this frosty night.
With every slip, and every laugh,
We'll celebrate our winter craft.

Whispers of Winter's Breath

A cough from winter, quite the tease,
Turns noses red, just like the trees.
With every gust, new shivers sprout,
And laughter follows, no one pouts.

An otter dives, does flips and spins,
While icy ponds bring cheeky grins.
But when he jumps, and lands with flair,
He finds a snowball stuck in hair!

The clouds conspired with frigid glee,
'They'll never spot us,' said the spree.
But a snowman sneezed, a frosty gale,
And off flew hats like feathers frail.

Come gather 'round, let's share a cheer,
For winter's shenanigans draw near.
With frosty breath and playful shouts,
We'll spin tales under stars, no doubts.

Glistening Secrets Beneath the White

Under white coats that look so bright,
Lies a laser tag course, what a sight!
Kids with masks, they run around,
In search of snowflakes that make no sound.

A dog slips past, thinks it's a game,
Digs for secrets, but finds no fame.
He rolls and tumbles with snowball glee,
While onlookers laugh, 'Oh what a spree!'

Snowflakes whisper as they glide,
Hiding behind trees with arms spread wide.
Each plop echoes a secret laugh,
'Let's surprise 'em with our winter craft!'

So here's to fun, beneath the freeze,
Where giggles tumble with such sweet ease.
We'll chase the mist, we'll sled in bands,
With smiles brightening these chilly lands.

Snowy Echoes and Whispered Wishes

A penguin slid past with a wink,
He thought he could dance, don't you think?
With flippers flailing, he took a great fall,
And left us all laughing, oh what a ball!

The snowflakes were giggling, a cacophony bright,
As squirrels donned hats, such a curious sight.
They chased after acorns, slipping in glee,
Creating a ruckus, oh did we agree!

A snowman with style, top hat and a grin,
Claimed he was fashion's first mannequin.
He posed and he preened, till a gust made him lean,
And down came his nose, what a humorous scene!

So we raised our hot cocoa, with marshmallows afloat,
To the laughter of winter, oh what a remote!
As echoes kept whispering through the chill air,
We found joy in the mishaps, beyond all compare.

When the World Glimmers with White

The sun peeked out, a rare sight today,
While snowball fights broke out, hip hip hooray!
With laughter and shouts, all were in the fray,
Dodging fluffy missiles, what a delight play!

A snowcat pranced by, with a snowy crown,
Swaggering proudly all over the town.
With each little step, he slipped in surprise,
And tumbled right down, to our great reprise!

The kids built a fort, oh what a grand scheme,
While plotting their raids, each hour, a dream!
But blueprints went awry, as a plow came by,
And buried their plans, oh my, oh my!

With mugs held aloft, we toasted the cold,
To fun in the frolic, and stories retold.
In laughter, we found warmth, as winter took flight,
In a world that glimmers, all feathery white.

Hours Lost in a Frozen Dreamscape

Slipping on paths, with a laugh and a squeal,
A grandma went gliding, quite a merry wheel.
Her cane became a toboggan, oh what a sight,
While grandkids all cheered in pure delight!

The air turned crisp, but our spirits were warm,
As we danced on the ice, dodging the swarm.
With every cute spin, the laughter did swell,
Till someone got dizzy and tripped, oh so well!

A deer donned a scarf, as if it were chic,
Strutting through snowdrifts, looking unique.
But tripped on a twig, a ballet gone wrong,
And tumbled through snowflakes, where it felt right
along!

We wrapped up the day with cocoa in hand,
Retelling our stories, as we made winter grand.
In hours lost here, the joy overflowed,
In this frozen dreamscape, where laughter still glowed.

The Heartbeat of Snow Underfoot

Crunching below, every step was a joke,
As kids chased the dogs, and laughter awoke.
With snowflakes like sprinkles on winter's slow cake,
We marveled at snowmen who started to shake.

A turtle in boots, with a swagger so free,
Mischievously gliding, oh who could foresee?
He fancied a race, and off he took flight,
But spun like a top, into a snowdrift, what a sight!

Snowball precision! The aim was on point,
Till someone screamed "friendly fire," a hilarious joint.
Allies turned foes in this winter delight,
And chuckles erupted, flourishing bright.

With hearts full of joy and snow in our hair,
We built and we laughed, with not a single care.
In this heartbeat of snow, we claimed our own cheer,
As winter became magic, year after year.

Secrets Beneath the Winter's Glow

Beneath the snow, where secrets hide,
A squirrel's stash is his pride.
He digs around with comic flair,
Finding acorns—oh, what a scare!

The snowflakes dance like tiny elves,
While we trudge on, lost in ourselves.
My boot, a trap for careless glee,
I'd swear it's laughing back at me!

The snowman's grin, so big and wide,
Hides the truth he cannot abide.
A carrot nose, a button eye,
He plots revenge against the sky!

So much to see beneath moon's glow,
With mittens stuck, we creep and toe.
The winter's laugh is loud and clear,
Grab your sled, the fun is near!

Glistening Adventures of the Heart

On a slope where snowballs fly,
A friendly face said, "Give it a try!"
But timing's key; just take the lead,
I launch a snowball, oh, what a speed!

With ice skates strapped, we whirl and spin,
Adventures on ice, where laughs begin.
But one little slip, and down I plop,
Like a penguin sliding, oh, what a drop!

We build a fort, our fortress grand,
Attracting snowballs from the neighboring band.
A laugh so loud, my cheeks a flush,
A snowball battle, oh, what a rush!

Under the stars, we'll share our dreams,
As snowflakes waltz in moonlit beams.
With giggles and grins, hearts all aglow,
Winter's adventures make the best show!

Journey Through the Crystal Wonderland

Oh look, a path, all shiny and bright,
A sledding trip seems just right.
But wait, a puddle? I take the leap,
Landed in snow like a giant heap!

A snow angel made, with style and grace,
A floppy hat, my new favorite place.
The world's a canvas, white and clean,
Till my dog jumps in, and ruins the scene!

The trees are dressed in icy crowns,
While we roll around like silly clowns.
With every tumble, I'm sure I'll find,
More treasures beneath, and more snow to grind!

Giggles burst forth on a chilly night,
We share stories that feel just right.
In this frosty realm, where laughter reigns,
A crystal wonderland, free of pains!

Memories Loomed in Winter's Hush

In winter's hush, we gather round,
To tell our tales, together bound.
But when I spoke, I lost my track,
Snowflakes fell and I fell back!

A cup of cocoa, oh so sweet,
Hold on tight, the fun's not complete.
With whipped cream hats, we take a sip,
But mine's a mustache—let it rip!

Snowball forts like castles stand,
We wage our war, it's quite the plan.
Yet from nowhere, my best friend threw,
A snowball avalanche! Oh no, it's true!

With laughter shared and memories spun,
In winter's warmth, we all have fun.
Wrapped in smiles and snowy cheer,
These moments felt, we hold so dear!

Shroud of White

A blanket thick, oh what a sight,
The dog thinks it's just pure delight.
He leaps, he bounds, a snowball spree,
Then slips on ice, oh poor puppy!

Kids scream as snowballs whiz on by,
The mom just laughs, oh me, oh my!
She joins the war, no time to fret,
But trips and lands, and now she's wet!

Snowmen rise with carrots for noses,
But one's head fell—who left those poses?
A twig for arms, dressed up just right,
But now he's just a sad snow sight!

Winter's joke, a frosty prank,
With laughter warm, we'll raise a tank!
For in this cold, laughs keep us bright,
As we trudge home through the pale twilight.

Cloak of Silence

Whispers hush in the leafy trees,
Snowflakes dance, a ghostly tease.
The squirrel's plop, a soft thud sound,
He hoped for grace, but slid around!

In winter's calm, I trip and yelp,
Who knew that ice could make you kelp?
My mittens soaked, I can't feel my hands,
Guess I'll build a house with snowy strands!

The path ahead looks like a slide,
My feet a-glide, I let fate decide.
But up ahead, a snowman's grin,
I squished his nose, and now he's thin!

Nature's chill has a funny twist,
From giggles here, it can't be missed.
So let's embrace this winter night,
Wrapped up warm, laughing with delight.

Beyond the Gates of a Winter Wonderland

A wreath of snow at every door,
Children dash, their laughter soar.
They build a fort, a palace grand,
Then slip and fall, they didn't plan!

The air is bracing, hearts are light,
But frostbite's nipping with all its might.
One brave soul says, "I'll take the dive!"
Splash in a puddle—now they thrive!

Mittens tossed, a playful spree,
Snowballs fly like wild confetti.
But watch your back, and guard your coat,
Here comes a penguin in a snowboat!

With mugs of cocoa, we share warm tales,
Of snowy mishaps and slippery trails.
Laughter echoes under the stars,
In this winter's world, fun-filled memoirs!

The Frosty Canvas of Nature's Art

A canvas bright, all white and fair,
Nature's brush left sparkles everywhere.
Snowflakes twirl like ballet feet,
But watch your step, don't take a seat!

Penguins waddling, looking absurd,
One took a tumble—oh how we heard!
With flails and flops, they steal the show,
Who knew ice could lead to such a flow?

A snowball fight, the stakes are clear,
Duck for cover, here comes the cheer!
But one round's missed, it hit the cat,
Now he's plotting a victory spat!

Oh winter's charm, with all its quirks,
Brings giggles out among the jerks.
As laughter spills in the chilly air,
We live for moments we all can share.

Winding Through Twilit Frost

Down winding paths, we drift and swerve,
The snowflakes tease, their charm they serve.
With every step, the crunch so dear,
Yet sometimes leads to quite a leer!

A tumble here, a roll through there,
Snow on the nose is quite a scare!
Like ballerinas tripping in white,
We tumble and giggle till it's night.

The trees dressed up with glistening coats,
Whisper secrets like chatty goats.
A frosty breeze tickles our nose,
Watch out for snowballs, here it goes!

So let us wander through this delight,
Where everything sparkles, oh so bright.
In the heart of chill, our spirits soar,
For in winter's grasp, we laugh and explore!

The Lure of Icy Meadows

In gardens white, where snowflakes play,
Little critters slide away.
A snowman built, with carrot nose,
Turns out to be a funny pose.

Sleds go flying, kids in a race,
One falls down, takes a face-plant grace.
Laughter echoes, joyful cries,
As snowballs fly and snowmen lie.

Mittens lost, and boots too tight,
Snowflakes swirl, oh what a sight!
They dance around in chilly cheer,
While warm cocoa waits near, oh dear!

The playtime ends as twilight falls,
With rosy cheeks and winter calls.
We'll dream of snow till springtime beams,
In our cozy homes, or so it seems.

When the World Wears a White Shroud

When morning breaks, the white is bright,
The dog darts out, no time for fright.
He sees the snow, a fluffy mound,
And promptly rolls, then spins around.

Kids bundled up, look like marshmallows,
Waddling out like chubby fellows.
They aim their snowballs, laughter loud,
And hit their dad, who's feeling proud.

Sleds derail, and oh what glee,
Mom sipping tea thinks, 'Let it be!'
On this winter wonderland spree,
We laugh and joke, feeling so free.

As night falls down, our cheeks aglow,
We share our tales of slippery show.
Warm by the fire, we chuckle bright,
At tales of woes in the snowy night.

Haunting Beauty of a Snow-clad Forest

The trees wear coats of sparkling white,
As creatures scurry, what a sight!
A squirrel slips, he tumbles down,
Then shakes it off, no hint of frown.

In the still woods, a snowflake lands,
Upon a nose of a toe-warmer's hands.
Birds chirp softly, as if to say,
'Who ordered winter for the day?'

A snowshoe hare makes a quick dash,
While frolicking kids make a big splash.
They twirl and twirl, in glee so loud,
Creating chaos, oh, they feel proud!

As the sun dips low, shadows grow long,
We sing silly songs, all cheerful and strong.
With memories made, we bid adieu,
Till next winter's charm brings us anew.

Glimmers of Hope Amidst the Cold

When winter's grip makes us all freeze,
Hot cocoa calls, 'Come! Take it with ease!'
We gather round, in fluffy attire,
A blaze of laughs, warmth we acquire.

The snowman wobbles, and what a sight,
He looks like he's had a fun-filled night.
With buttons mismatched, a hat askew,
He's quite the character, that much is true!

A playful pup in a fluffy hat,
Chases his tail, oh where's it at?
And sledding down that bumpy hill,
We giggle hard, we can't sit still!

In the quiet night, stars start to peek,
Out in the snow, we hear laughter peek.
Hope shines bright, as we find our way,
In winter's embrace, we choose to play.

Frosty Imprints of a Sacred Journey

The boots I wore, a shade too tight,
Left prints of laughter, oh what a sight!
Each step a jig, a clumsy twirl,
Snowballs launched in a frantic whirl.

A penguin slid past, gave me a wink,
I tripped on an ice patch—what did I think?
With every tumble and flurry of snow,
I chuckled aloud at my tragic show.

The map I brought claimed to be wise,
But led me to where the snowman lies.
As I tried to bow, my hat took flight,
A chill in the air, a comical fright.

With each frosty breath, I felt so spry,
Yet, I lost my mitten and said, "Oh my!"
I chased it down, the snowflakes in dance,
Winter's laughter—a wild romance.

Reflections in a Winter's Mirror

The pond looked like glass, so shiny and neat,
I donned my skates, oh, what a feat!
But one little slip had me pirouette,
In a blizzard ballet I'll never forget.

My friends all cheered as they sipped hot tea,
"Look at him go, so fancy and free!"
But down I went with an icy splat,
Turns out a snowman is a much better chat.

The shovels were out, a raucous bouquet,
We built a grand fort in a glorious way.
But when it collapsed, oh, what a mess,
We laughed 'til we cried, no time to obsess.

With mittens like bricks, we staged a snow fight,
Snowballs flew left, oh what a delight!
Covered in snow, we rolled with glee,
In winter's embrace, such joy, wild and free.

The Veil of Ice Over Forgotten Places

Once a grand path, now a frozen joke,
With branches waving, like a mischievous cloak.
I slid through bushes, my dignity gone,
A squirrel just chuckled, "What's taking so long?"

With icy fingers, I reached for my phone,
To capture the chaos, yet felt quite alone.
But alas, it slipped and danced off the rail,
A moment of silence—a companion, a fail.

The old bench was there, wrapped snug in white,
I attempted a seat, but what a fright!
It creaked loud and nestled me deep,
I laughed so hard, I forgot to peep.

The mailman shuffled with rhythm and grace,
But slipped on a patch, what a grand race!
In the realm of ice, let laughter abound,
In the jests of a winter, joy can be found.

Glittering Veils of the Nocturnal Sky

Beneath the stars, the moon shone bright,
We wandered in wonder, oh what a night!
With twinkling helmets, our heads donned in glee,
We danced like goofballs, just wild and free.

Snowflakes surrendered, so soft like a kiss,
We caught them all—sweet frosty bliss!
But one drifted down and landed on my nose,
A little reminder of where winter goes.

As twilight painted the world in white,
We built a snow castle, oh what a sight!
With turrets and towers, or so we supposed,
But it leaned to the side—hilarious and dozed.

An owl flew by, gave me a stare,
"Is that your creation?" I could only glare.
But with every misstep, laughter took flight,
In winter's embrace, everything feels right.

Chasing Shadows on Icy Breezes

On slippery slopes, we take our chance,
With flailing arms, it's a silly dance.
Snowballs fly with mischievous glee,
As laughter echoes through each frosty tree.

Sleds zoom by like rockets in flight,
We giggle and tumble, what a sight!
Snowmen watch with a buttoned glare,
While igloos groan beneath the weight of care.

Sudden wipeouts, oh, what a splash!
Winter wishes we'd all take a crash.
Yet even in falls, joy is the creed,
We bounce back up, fueled by the speed.

So here we frolic, with cheeks all aglow,
Chasing each other through the white below.
With snowflakes swirling and spirits so bright,
We'll conquer the winter, oh what a night!

In the Footfalls of Winter Spirits

In the hush of the woods, we trek with glee,
Footprints behind lead to mystery.
Each crackling twig underfoot does sing,
As we dance with snowmen, they bring us bling.

We stumble on ice, like penguins in flight,
A wobbly ballet, oh what a sight!
The trees gossip low, their branches in cheer,
As we plop in the snow, without any fear.

Cocoa spills warm, on wobbly knees,
While snowflakes tease us with gentle sneezes.
Winter whispers secrets, giggles a tune,
As we dodge chilly sprites beneath the moon.

With laughter as thick as the snow we crave,
We summon the spirits, so silly and brave.
For in every flake that lands on the ground,
There's joy and mischief eternally found!

Hushed Steps in the Frozen Wilds

On a frosty morn, we tiptoe, we creep,
Through fields of powder, where snow bunnies leap.
Each silent step squelches, a giggly surprise,
As frost nips at toes, oh, how time flies!

Mittens tangled, we throw up the white,
When snow angels flop, it's a comical sight.
With every soft flop, there's a jubilant shout,
Funny faces made, as we roll all about.

Icicles jingle like bell chimes on trees,
The wind plays tricks, oh, it's all just a tease.
A snowball whizzes—oh, duck for your life!
Winter's a prankster, but leads us to strife.

Yet in every tumble, we find pure delight,
With rosy-cheeked giggles that dance in the night.
In the quiet of winter, let joy take its sway,
For laughter's the warmth that will brighten our day!

A Journey Through the Haunting Cold

In the ghostly mist, we wander and roam,
With snowflakes as maps leading us home.
A snowman grins with a carrot-y nose,
While wind howls a tune that nobody knows.

Flurries swirl, like a ball in the air,
As we slip on the ice, our best ballet flair.
With hearts full of joy and cheeks rosy bright,
We chase after shadows that dance in the night.

The chill is a joker, it plays tricks on toes,
But each frozen giggle, the spirit bestows.
Sliding through drifts, we're the kings of the hill,
In the snow-covered kingdom, time stands still.

So raise up your mugs filled with hot cocoa cheer,
For the magic of winter is really quite dear.
With warmth in our hearts, and a twinkle in mind,
We'll trek through the cold, leaving no fun behind!

The Serenity of a Snow-Blanketed World

The world wrapped in white, oh what a sight,
Snowflakes dance down, making ground feel light.
In mittens I trip, then slip on my rear,
A winter ballet, with giggles I cheer.

The trees wear their coats, all snuggly and round,
While snowmen conspire to roll on the ground.
With carrot and coal, they grin with delight,
Waving their sticks, giddy with winter's bite.

The silence is thick, like a marshmallow treat,
Each crunch underneath is a snow-shoeing beat.
I make my grand snow angel, flop down with a splash,
My wings turn to flippers, oh what a crash!

Yet as I get up, all covered in snow,
My imagination starts to twinkle and glow.
In this winter wonder, I laugh away woes,
For joy in the chill, oh it readily grows.

Traces of Magic in the Frigid Air

In the chill of the wind, where icicles creep,
I tried to build snow forts, but just made a heap.
A snowball was launched, but oh what a fail,
It landed on Max, my friend with a wail.

The squirrels in the trees, they backflip and spin,
While I'm there just bundled, trying to win.
Running like penguins, we shuffle and slide,
To avoid the next snowball that's launched far and wide.

I spot a small snowdrift, my throne for the day,
But I tumble right back and I roll all the way.
With laughter erupting, the neighbors all stare,
At a grown-up caught giggling, lost in mid-air.

Hot cocoa awaits, with marshmallows piled,
Each sip is a treasure, winter's secret compiled.
In the frosty embrace, we find joy and cheer,
For nothing's more magical than winter, my dear.

An Odyssey Across the Winter's Breath

The world is a canvas, in colors so bright,
But my nose is so red, I could give Rudolph fright.
With boots made for stomping, I wade through the snow,
Leaving footprints like giant, confused buffalo.

I thought I'd go sledding, oh what a great plan,
But my sled just went sideways, like I was in a van.
With each wild twist and turn, I squeal with pure glee,
It's like an amusement park, just for me!

Frosty breezes tickle my ears and my chin,
Creating snow sculptures, let the chaos begin!
A diabolical snowman, with a smile so broad,
Looks suspiciously like my neighbor, oh my God!

The sky turns to twilight, a pastel display,
We laugh, we regain, as we get carried away.
With cheeks all a-flush and spirits so high,
We wave to the night, as the stars start to fly.

Celestial Patterns in the Snow

I wander through winters with snowflakes in hand,
Drawing doodles and hearts in this bubbly white land.
My plans for a snowball surprisingly turned,
Into cheeks pelted, much to my concern.

The frost in the air gives my nose quite a chill,
Yet warmth in my belly grows, oh what a thrill!
We fashion a snow beast, an impressive high mound,
With googly eyes winking, perplexing the ground.

The sun plays peek-a-boo through clouds soft and gray,
Making topsy-turvy shadows as we tumble and play.
Our laughter erupts, a melody sweet,
While we dance on the white in our cozy snow feet.

When the evening draws close, and the stars twinkle
bright,
I'll sip on my cocoa, all toasty and light.
In this whimsical world, where winter's our friend,
We cherish the moments that never will end.

Beneath the White

Under the blanket so fluffy and bright,
Squirrels are plotting, oh what a sight!
They hide their acorns, each one a delight,
While I just trip over, not quite upright.

Snowmen are laughing with carrot-nose glee,
As I slip and slide, oh what fun for me!
They wave their twig arms, so jolly, so free,
While I tumble down, wishing for tea!

Goggles and mittens, a fashion faux pas,
Yet here I am, stylish—ha! Not a clue,
With every small step, I'm courting a fall,
But hey, there's a snowball fight waiting for you!

So here in the winter, I stumble and roll,
With laughter erupting, it warms up my soul.
Beneath the white cover, I find my new goal,
To dance through the flurries, and that's how I stroll!

Memories Drift

In the quiet of winter, with sleds piled high,
We zoom down the hill, and woosh! I fly!
But forgotten my brakes, oh where do they lie?
Smack into a snowdrift, and now I can't cry!

Snowflakes are curious, they flutter and tease,
As I waddle outside, in search of some cheese.
Catch one on my tongue, oh how it does freeze,
A popsicle treat, and yet I still sneeze!

The dog steals my mittens, all fluffy and white,
He thinks they are snacks, oh what a sly bite!
Now we're both laughing, in one goofy fight,
While the snow falls around us, it's pure delight!

But eventually twilight, the day starts to fade,
I head back indoors, the fun never strayed.
I'll dream of the laughter and snowy parade,
A tale full of memories, I gladly relayed!

The Soft Touch of Winter's Kiss

Winter whispers softly, a chuckle in tone,
As I tackle the shovel, oh how it has grown!
The driveway's a mountain, a glacier-like throne,
Yet here comes my cat, she claims it as home.

With floppy earmuffs, I venture outside,
Only to find the snowmen collide!
A pom-pom off one, a boot on the side,
Ah, the antics unfold, my grin cannot hide!

My scarf flies away, a kite in a breeze,
I chase after it, oh please, don't you tease!
A snowball flies past—who threw that with ease?
A laugh erupts loud as I try not to freeze!

In the still of the evening, a wonder takes hold,
Frozen laughter dances, a secret foretold.
Beneath the cold sky, my heart's never bold,
In winter's quick humor, its warmth I behold!

Drifting into a Snowy Reverie

As I wander about, my thoughts start to glide,
A snow-covered world, I take in with pride.
But one slip and tumble, I'm off for a ride,
Down the hill sideways, oh how I abide!

The squirrels give chase, what right do they have?
With nuts in their cheeks, they laugh as I staved.
They gather in clusters, all smug and so brave,
While I'm just a marshmallow, in need of a salve!

A snow angel flaps from my aching arm's grace,
Yet land on a patch that's all icy with lace.
Now I'm stuck in a pose, a wintry disgrace,
They point at my floundering with joy on their face!

So here I am lost, in snow-swept delight,
With laughter and grumbles, I bid you goodnight.
In the memory of winter, so full of bright light,
Each trip in the snow is a whimsical flight!

Chronicles of Ice Beneath a Dull Sun

Under a gray sky, the ice charms the ground,
But here comes my buddy, he's slipping around!
He aims for the snowbank, but oh, how he's bound,
With a flip and a flop, down he goes with a sound!

We gather our courage and challenge the flat,
To skate on the puddles, oh look, here comes Matt!
He wobbles and flails, but then there's a spat,
Dancing ducks quack loudly, "This man is a brat!"

So armed with our boots, we venture forth wide,
To pillow the snowbanks as laughter resides.
Yet somehow, it seems the snow just collided,
With principles of physics, no gold medalists!

But still we persist, in this wintry embrace,
For all of our blunders, we find grace in this place.
With stories of mischief, a smile on my face,
We toast to this season—let's keep up the chase!

Crystalline Dreams beneath Silver Skies

Snowflakes tumble, doing a dance,
They pirouette, oh what a chance!
A squirrel slips in a comical whirl,
While snowman grins, sporting a twirl.

Icicles dangle, sharp and bright,
They threaten hats in a snowy fight.
With every chuckle, we slip and slide,
Chasing the winter, our laughter wide.

Hot cocoa spills, a marshmallow's fate,
All's fun and games until it's too late!
We stumble and fall, against nature's pride,
In winter's embrace, joy can't be denied.

So bring on the laughter, let spirits soar,
In this frozen land, who could ask for more?
A frosty jest, a chilly pun,
In crystalline dreams, we all have fun!

Twilight's Kiss on a Snowy Canvas

Twilight settles with a playful grin,
Whispers of snowflakes, let the fun begin!
A dog dashes past, chasing its tail,
On a snowy canvas, it never will fail.

A family builds a fortress so grand,
With snowball ammo at ready hand.
Sudden ambush! A brother yells loud,
As snowballs fly, laughter's the crowd.

The snowman wears a scarf and a hat,
He's the fashion king, where the cold is at!
But wait! A gentle breeze starts to tease,
Off goes his hat, caught in the trees!

Twilight lingers, but spirits stay bright,
In the snowy world, every snowflake's light.
With giggles and joy, we twist and spin,
In evening's blush, winter's fun will win!

Shadows in the Winter Light

Under the sun, shadows play tricks,
As we leap around like frosty flicks.
With feet in snow, we make a few leaps,
And laughter echoes as the sunlight creeps.

Welcome to winter, a season of glee,
Where hot soup might just be a frisbee!
A sledding mishap, a tumble, a roll,
In every mistake, we're losing control.

Flurries dance like a waltz misled,
While a snowball war's on, swift as lead.
A mitten flies off through the frosty air,
As we chase it down without a care.

Shadows grow long, but we're not quite done,
In this winter play, every second's fun.
With laughter and love, we melt the cold night,
In shadows of winter, hearts take flight!

Melodies of Frozen Streams

Frozen streams hum a sweet icy tune,
With every step, they whistle to the moon.
A deer prances by wearing a crown,
Of frosty jewels, no frown to be found.

Chirping birds don their winter attire,
While we bumble forth, a snowy choir.
A slip here and there, oh what fun,
With laughter exploding, no care for the run!

Sideways we ski, on a haywire path,
Collecting snow as we plunge with a laugh.
A snowflake tickles the end of my nose,
A giggle erupts, how ridiculous it grows!

Melodies chime as we dance in delight,
In this chilly realm, where nothing feels right.
Beneath the cold glimmer, laughter rings clear,
In the music of winter, joy hovers near!

Enchanted Treads on Icy Ground

Slipping and sliding, we dash like a deer,
Laughing so hard, we can't help but cheer.
With each little stumble, we turn into clowns,
In this frosty wonderland, laughter abounds.

Snowballs are flying, a flurry of fun,
Dodging our friends, oh, how we run!
With mittens on hands and snowsuits so bright,
We whirl through the park, what a hilarious sight!

Mittens entwined, we keep losing our grip,
A cascade of giggles with each hilarious trip.
Chasing our shadows, we tumble and play,
This slippery ballet makes for a grand day!

When the sun sets low, and the sky turns to grey,
We'll search for hot cocoa to sip on our way.
For nothing is better than laughter and cheer,
In this icy domain we hold so dear.

Serene Wanderings in Winter's Realm

In a land wrapped in white, I slip and fall,
Bouncing back up, I'm having a ball.
A yeti appears, or so I believe,
Turns out it's just my friend, dressed to deceive!

Snowflakes are twirling, like children on swings,
We prance through the drifts, imagining kings.
With snowpants so bulky, we waddle like ducks,
Who knew winter's armor could bring in such luck?

A squirrel steals my snack, oh what a sly chap,
I chase after it, right into the flap!
We tangle and tumble, laughing in glee,
Who would have thought snow could so wild be?

When evening descends, we build us a fort,
With cupcakes on guard, our sweet little sport.
In this winter wonder, it's happiness found,
As we frost the entire world with giggles abound.

A Dance of Snowflakes in the Breeze

Like a ballet of chaos, the snowflakes do play,
Twisting and turning in their own special way.
We pirouette clumsily, laughing with glee,
Only to tumble, 'that's how it should be!'

A snowman stands tall, but my nose has gone rogue,
It rolls like a ball, now it's a snowdog!
With carrot for nose, it begins to zoom,
Chasing away laughter, right into the gloom.

Snowballs ignite, as the battle begins,
Faces get splattered, oh where are my bins?
With pockets of snow, we throw without care,
Where laughter erupts, you might find a bear!

The sun starts to set, glowing warm and bright,
We wobble and tumble, enchanted by light.
For in this grand dance, laughter's the prize,
As we skip from the slopes, under starry skies.

The Chill of Forgotten Journeys

Once a path I followed, now lost in the haze,
With powdery snow filling up all the bays.
Forgotten are footsteps, they slip right away,
Just like my wallet, they've gone on holiday!

My boots are enchanted, or so they would seem,
They glide over ice like I'm living a dream.
With a flip and a flop, and my bear-like grace,
I'm spinning in circles, lost in this race!

As I dive in the snow, it's not what I planned,
A snow turtle emerges, it's more than I can stand.
We laugh at the antics, while snowflakes conspire,
To blanket the ground in their frosty attire.

Yet memories linger of journeys long past,
With friends by my side, oh, how they abound!
We'll fill the cold nights with stories and jest,
In winter's cool grasp, we'll warm up the best.

Milton Keynes UK
Ingram Content Group UK Ltd.
UKHW022006131124
451149UK00013B/1037